Unfading Rhapsodies

P. Mary Vidya Porselvi

A Journey Through Life, Love, and the Lyric Soul

BLUEROSE PUBLISHERS
India | U.K.

Copyright © P.Mary Vidya Porselvi 2025

All rights reserved by author. No part of this publication may be reproduced, stored in a retrieval system or transmitted in any form or by any means, electronic, mechanical, photocopying, recording or otherwise, without the prior permission of the author. Although every precaution has been taken to verify the accuracy of the information contained herein, the publisher assume no responsibility for any errors or omissions. No liability is assumed for damages that may result from the use of information contained within.

BlueRose Publishers takes no responsibility for any damages, losses, or liabilities that may arise from the use or misuse of the information, products, or services provided in this publication.

For permissions requests or inquiries regarding this publication, please contact:

BLUEROSE PUBLISHERS
www.BlueRoseONE.com
info@bluerosepublishers.com
+91 8882 898 898
+4407342408967

ISBN: 978-93-7018-202-8

Cover design: Daksh
Typesetting: Tanya Raj Upadhyay

First Edition: May 2025

To

Amma and Appa

PREFACE

Ray Bradbury in 'Zen in the Art of Writing' notes, "Be pragmatic, then. If you are not happy with the way your writing has gone, you might give my method a try. If you do, I think you might easily find a new definition for Work. And the word is LOVE."

'Unfading Rhapsodies' is born out of **LOVE** (*Anbu*). The collection is my earnest endeavor to pen down my honest expressions of memorable "love" moments in lines of verse. It represents a spectrum of feelings and emotions, garnered within tranquil capsule moments…each one captured in simple poetic lines, crafted amidst the hustle and bustle of daily life and challenging work schedules. This book offers a bouquet of varied feelings and emotions… ecstasy, rapture, sublimity, and sobriety—each woven together to magically reveal my love and respect for nature, culture, society, people, places, and the Divine.

Just as music embraces the universe with its diversity and the power of integrative imagination, the 105 poems in this anthology vary widely in form, theme, tone, and style classified under the following titles: Pitch for Green Leaves, Timbre in Brown Bark, Texture of Blue Skies, Dynamics of Gold Sun, Tempo in Teal Plumes, Rhythm of Red Roses, Harmony in Black Woods, Melody of Purple Petals, Beat to Silver Streams and Meter of White Clouds.

The work humbly attempts to align itself with the Romantic poetic tradition inspired by William Wordsworth's timeless definition of poetry as "the spontaneous overflow of powerful feelings," and equally influenced by the spiritual insights of the seer poet Rabindranath Tagore, who embraces the mystery of "utterances ineffable."

At this juncture of my poetic quest, I strongly believe that writing (I would like to call) is "**ZENNEY**," a portmanteau of **Zen Journey** between the interior world (*Akam*) and the exterior world (*Puram*). The book extends a warm invitation to the readers to relish the conscious, hand-picked words, the potent pauses in between the words, elusive ellipses, and silences in lines, and, find meaning also, in the unsaid. From traditional sonnets, odes and somber elegies to simple and unassuming haikus, lyrical pieces set to music, free verse, and bold experimental patterns, the collection truly represent the mad to meditative Zen Journey.

Theoretically, the three stages of the Zen journey or Zenney identified in this meaning-making process are: Poetic Indulgence, Poetic Immanence, and Poetic Transcendence.

On a day-to-day mundane routine, a person, place, or thing, the fragrance of a flower, the aroma of food, the music that travels across in a gentle breeze can connect with our soul on different levels. It can affect us for a second, a minute, an hour, a day or for eternity. It can alter our psyche forever. **Poetic Indulgence** is an expression I have coined to describe the creative thought spark moment when a person is carried away/jolted by an authentic, spontaneous experience in the exterior world (*Puram*) which s/he tries to relish, protect, cherish and sustain in her/his heart, mind, and soul in the interior world (*Akam*) over a period with a purpose of creating works of art that result in an alternative imaginary cosmos of love, hope, freedom, and peace.

In the process, the writer gets immersed into nature and culture at different levels. This stage I would like to define as **Poetic Immanence** in the Zen journey. Depending upon the emotions, feelings, energy, vibration, and frequency exerted on the thoughts and actions, the immanence can be seen as a representation of an experience ranging from a few seconds or minutes to a decade or a century. Poetic Immanence adds value to the poetic subjects beyond imagination where: the ordinary becomes extraordinary; the mundane becomes surreal; the human becomes superhuman; and the natural becomes supernatural.

Poetry enables humans to develop the intuitive, integrative power to connect the dots between the different aspects of nature and culture which I would like to call, the **Poetic Transcendence**. The poetic transcendence depends upon the height, depth, and width of love (*Anbu*) as a unifying factor with which the writer is capable of perception with sensitivity; reflection with clarity; and understanding with depth to mindfully re-create his/her poetic cosmos in relation to the real world. Unlike the traditional, privileged, dominant systems that define transcendence as "otherworldly," for a woman writer, the poetic transcendence akin to Simone de Beauvoir's ideas on existentialism, is deeply rooted within immanence, like a Bodhi tree redefining the "divine existence" or "the state of grace" within the day-to-day experience of life.

Unfading Rhapsodies is more than a collection of poems. It is an exploratory Zen Journey in three stages: indulgence, immanence, and transcendence that celebrates life, beauty, and the quiet miracles that surrounds us when we take a moment to truly see, feel, and listen with love and care in our hearts (*Akam*).

I am grateful to my first set of poetic audience, my Appa Packiaraj, my Amma Nirmala, my sister Priya, my brother Jai, my husband Roy Arun, my sons Amal, and Iniyan whose enthusiasm and constant encouragement made this work possible. I am thankful to my teachers, students, research scholars, friends, and colleagues for their candid remarks and, at times, pointblank, critical feedback that always inspires me to write more.

P. Mary Vidya Porselvi

Table of Contents

I   Pitch for Green Leaves 1
    1. Leaves are Roots in Green 1
    2. An Ode to *Thamizh* 2
    3. Onam in Austin 3
    4. Madurai 6
    5. An Emotion That Found Words 8
    6. Coffee Tales 9
    7. Thaai Mama 15
    8. A Trip Down the Memory Lane 18
    9. In a World Fraught with Pain 21
    10. She Ached in Happiness 23

II   Timbre in Brown Bark 24
    11. Birthday at Madison 24
    12. Kurinci 26
    13. Mullai 27
    14. Marutam 28
    15. Neytal 29
    16. Palai 30
    17. Bus Journey to Vettavalam 31
    18. Mother Earth T-r-e-m-o-r-s 34
    19. Child Earth – An Alphabet Poem 35
    20. Mary Knew Him 38

III   Texture of Blue Skies 41
    21. Haiku in Love 41
    22. Breathlessness 42

23.	Melted Like Ice 43
24.	High Walls 44
25.	So Many Tears 45
26.	Love in a Shell 46
27.	Graceful Glances 47
28.	Rock Bottom 48
29.	Metamorphosis 49
30.	She Had Seen His Regal Soul 50

IV Dynamics of Gold Sun 51
31.	Time Fools 51
32.	Equalizer 52
33.	A Mother's Prayer 53
34.	Life Leaves, Death Leaves 55
35.	Tree *Anni* 56
36.	Blending and Parting 58
37.	Unpredictable Divine 59
38.	Ma Buddha 61
39.	Within Four Walls 62
40.	Mother Tree 64

V Tempo in Teal Plumes 66
41.	Curry Leaves in Ziplock Pouch 66
42.	Family Reunion – A Prime Poem 68
43.	Water Un-homed 70
44.	Blue Ticks 71
45.	Word Child 72
46.	Mélange 73
47.	Words Heal 74
48.	To the Best of the Best 77

49.	Why Read Moby-Dick?	79
50.	Fasting is Feasting	82

VI Rhythm of Red Roses 83

51.	Inland Letters	83
52.	Mad Musings	85
53.	Eyes Never Lie	87
54.	Figures of Silence	88
55.	Tea for the Soul	89
56.	Winter Solstice	90
57.	Plant Love	91
58.	May the Day	92
59.	Flowers are Silent Prayers	93
60.	Gifts	94

VII Harmony in Black Woods 95

61.	sTree	95
62.	When I Die Don't Bury Me	96
63.	Saint of the Slums	97
64.	Life Sentence	98
65.	Bitter Sweet	100
66.	She Began Fasting	102
67.	Lingua Myopia	103
68.	Love Gift-Wrapped in Memory	104
69.	Breaking the Walls	106
70.	Tiny Little Particles of You	108

VIII Melody of Purple Petals 109

71.	Thorn Crowns	109
72.	Oh…!	110
73.	Distant Cousins	111

	74. Tears are Uncountable Words 112
	75. Where There is Divine Light 113
	76. Window in the Attic 115
	77. Nature's Fury 117
	78. Mettā Tunes of Gaia 118
	79. Anam Cara(Soul Friend) 119
	80. She Chose Silence 120

IX Beat to Silver Streams 122
    81. Mother Dear 122
    82. A Beacon of Wisdom 123
    83. Maya and Her Muse 124
    84. The Little Black Bird 125
    85. I am Home 126
    86. Birthing 127
    87. Refuge 128
    88. Magni-Psalm 130
    89. Bird Song 131
    90. Her Lord, Her Boss 132

X Meter of White Clouds 133
    91. Martians and Venusians 133
    92. Muse Soul 134
    93. Sober Silence 135
    94. Jesus of Nazareth 136
    95. King of Kings 137
    96. Ellipsis Psalm 138
    97. Chocolate Mothers 139
    98. Ration Shop 140
    99. Town Bus 141

100. Feathered Mother 142
101. Pollution 143
102. A Kind Word 144
103. Lucky Dip 145
104. Delhi Beckons 146
105. Find Her Deep Soul 147

I   Pitch for Green Leaves

1.   Leaves are Roots in Green

Leaves are roots in gentle green
that hold onto soil through veins,

scooping a bouquet of sunshine,
in their little pink tender palms,
like a newborn child in arms…

…of the Mother Nature Divine

2. An Ode to *Thamizh*

Soul
of our *thaai mozhi*,
Thamizh mozhi lives in *zha* like
deep and wide *aazhi* that surrounds us
beyond borderless boundaries

ancient giant *yazh* with mellifluous tunes
before Time's birth, renditioning herstories

benevolent *mazhai* mirroring human hearts
in the quintessential land of love and courage

where the ruler and the ruled uphold *thaazhchi*
and fear conscience to those who find refuge

with unprecedented glory in every *vaazhthu*
sung by young and old in praise of Mother

shows *nalvazhi* of justice and goodwill to many
from near and far, who faithfully harbour
and
soul of our *thaai mozhi*,
Thamizh mozhi lives in
zha

Celebration of the Tamil Letter/Sound 'Zha' as the soul of Tamil language, literature and culture.

3. Onam in Austin

Young Longhorn Mahabalis
in white *Veshtis*
and burnt-orange silk cotton shirts,
sing songs in praise of
auspicious beginnings.
Indian American women
in off-white *Kasavu* and stone *Jimikis*
prepare a giant *Pookalam*
on a round teak table with
colorful paper petals.

Remembering the ten days
harvest festival of
God's own country
after a hiatus of fasting
in the foreign shores
we end up having
a *Sadya* on a giant
Banana look-alike paper leaf,

beginning sincerely with
a pinch of salt,
crunchy, jaggery-dipped
Sharkaravaratti
that has traveled all the way from Home,

an appetizing tangy-sour
tamarind and ginger chutney,
faithfully followed by
thinly sliced Yam chips
mixed with boiled spices
and fried in virgin coconut oil,

Beans-Carrot *Pachadi* with juicy ginger
and fragrant curry leaves,
classic *Olan* slow-sim cooked
with Texan readymade coconut milk,
mixed vegetables stir fried
with grated coconut flakes
to form *Thoran*,

Mexican Moringa, Plantain *Avial*
carefully cooked in Chechi's style
with curd and coconut paste,

Earthy-Orange Pumpkins that do
not make it to Halloween
end up meeting red beans
in *Erissery*,

oil-dripping lime and mango pickle
in velvety royal brown hues that may
inspire the calorie-conscious crew,
a jogging around the Ladybird Lake,

ginger married to yogurt
to form classic pair *Inji Thayir*,

boiled lentils and shallots *Sambhar*
in comfort zone
with parboiled red rice,

little Ammu's favorite,
deep fried *Pappadams*
that had perfectly puffed up
without hitting fire alarms on rooftops,

and the delectable journey
ends up with the divine
Paal Ada pradhaman
and *Pazha pradhaman*
to recreate a soulful paradise

in every heart, hearth, and the Earth.

Remembering Onam Celebration and Sadya at the University of Texas at Austin in Fall 2019

Published in Amaranth journal - Autumn 2024 /Vol 3, Issue 2

4. Madurai

Just before sunrise
early morning breeze
from Azhagar Malai
wakes me up from deep slumber
amidst misty windows when
Pandiyan Express
crosses Sholavandan,

and my heart leaps with joy
as we head towards
the *Cankam* capital
in all her ancient glory,

where historical mahals
with giant archways and pillars
compete with modern day malls
to grasp children's attention
during summer vacation.

Roads effortlessly bordered
with heady fragrance of
jasmine flower shops at dawn
and sizzling hot
idli - dosai shops at dusk
drowns us deep down
with warmth,

like ever-flooded Vaigai river
besides Meenakshi Amman
in her royal throne
garbed in green silk saree
with mango and fish motifs
and matching emerald nose-pin

with hearts that speak
a language of incessant love
spiced with "*Anney*" and "*Akka*"
from all four directions

that provides soulful refuge
like cool cucumber clusters
and zingy *Jigarthanda*
on a hot sunny day in May.

Published in Muse India – the literary E-Journal
May-June 2023

5. An Emotion That Found Words

An emotion that tied
millions mildly together
with words of stern promise

to liberate sleepy souls

from slumber of ignorance
from temper of arrogance
from whimper of innocence

awakening them with
whip cracks of wisdom
translated into myriad vistas

as hope of the hopeless
as voice of the voiceless

to enlighten dark liminal paths
to enliven dizzy confused minds
to enrich dull dreary lives

with acts of promise

as searing seeds of faith
that nurtured, nourished, emerged
perennial trees of goodwill

along giant avenues of aspiration.

Dedicated to Babasaheb Dr Ambedkar and his contribution on April 14th 2023

6. Coffee Tales

I

On an eco-study tour

in a tribal settlement in
Kodaikanal

woman with native nose-pin
and crumpled cotton saree
donated by a local NGO

sits outside her thatched hut
and grinds soaked
dark beans in *Ammi*.

As we walk down
the rocky path famished
she asks us with a sublime smile

"Kaapi Thanni saaptreengala"

II

On a Monday morning

at my home in the 1980s

Amma gives me a tumbler
of coffee filled to brim.

Sleepily I drop it down
like a tender fledgling.

Amma busy polishing our
white canvas shoes hurriedly
looks up, and gives a long, long stare
and utters, "you always do this."

My eyes dam with tears
not at her words
but at the loss of coffee

Amma goes to the kitchen
and returns with another
tumbler of coffee filled to the brim

she had saved for herself.

III

On a Friday evening

in a crowded bus in the 1990s

A nurse sits next to me
and starts talking.

As the bus crosses T Nagar,
aroma of freshly ground coffee
wafts around in thick air

and sweeps us by storm

She fondly recollects,
that someone special
she had cared for
had once told her,

"When I recover and go home
I will invite you
to my hometown.
I will serve you
the best homegrown coffee"

Her eyes were filled with tears.
when she muttered,

"She never recovered."

IV

On a Sunday morning

in my ancestral village house

my cousin's girl-seeing function.
She holds out a tray of
Bhajji and Kesari with
special coffee mixed
with fresh milk
from cow Mangalam
in the backyard.

Her would be mother-in-law
asks her "Did you make this coffee?"
Without any hesitation
my cousin nods her head
in agreement and winks at me.

A year later

with morning sickness
when she craves for coffee,
her husband admonishes her
"Don't drink coffee now.
My child may turn out dark.
Drink juice instead"

she drank juice
and the child was born

in shiny coffee bean tone.

V

On a dark moon-lit night

In my mother-in-law's house

before cleaning up
kitchen tables
the grey-haired woman

faithfully boils some water
and drenches heaps
of coffee powder
in a brass filter.

In the morning, she loyally
serves the first decoction
to her husband and sons.
Then she pours some more water
in the already doused
pitiful mess
that has lost color
and flavor long time ago.

It was meant for women
of the household.
My heart screams at disparities.
I genuinely wish she had

the first decoction coffee someday.

VI

A day before the international conference

at midnight

I hear girls and boys shrieking
sirens blowing, lights flashing

afraid to look out of

the French window
from the hotel room
I play some soft
Ilayaraja music
and try to go to sleep
but remain awake
throughout the night.

Next morning
I curiously enquire
the receptionist Mia,
a student of the nearby university.

In a pleasant tone she clarifies
"That was a wedding party!
Were you disturbed!
We apologize for your
inconvenience.
Please do cheer up with some
Cappuccino or Cinnamon Latte"
and hands over a complementary

10 Dollar Starbucks coupon with a smile.

Part IV and V published in Muse India – the literary E-Journal May-June 2023

7. Thaai Mama

Your effervescent smile
and warm, caring words
with every line you spoke
ending with "ma" …

what a beautiful word
in Tamil *"Thaai Mama"* or *"Ammaan"*
a male cohort to *amma*
with unconditional love
that knows no boundaries.

In my II std class
when my teacher asked me
to describe my "favorite person"
I wrote about you…

as a wide-eyed little girl
during summer vacations
admiring you as a super star
in the leather jacket
I would accompany you
on early morning walks
amidst mist and fog…

you would tread

so fast up-hill
I would run behind you frantically
huffing and puffing
to catch up.

Holding your warm hands
and looking at
the sun rising above
misty-mighty mountains

listening to mynahs chirping,
smelling the dewy eucalyptus trees
was such a delectable treat

A dozen children,
yours and your siblings together
of all shapes and sizes
created innocent mayhem
every May month
and you treated us with grace.
Never have we seen
a frown on your face.

Time and space
can take you away from us.

But you will live in our hearts
as long as the sun rises

gloriously above
misty-mighty mountains
with mynahs cheerily-chirping
among the dewy eucalyptus trees
of our childhood haven Kodai.

For my maternal uncle Raj Mama's Birthday March 1st 2023 after he left us during the pandemic.

8. A Trip Down the Memory Lane

Shy, timid, but curious
we would enter an enchanted
world of wordsmiths
and take a quick deep dive
into the unfathomable sea
of ideas and imagination,

coaxed by our guardian angel
who was crazy about
laddus, pradhaman
Simone de Beauvoir and Sartre
and above all her darling students,
an enthusiastic busy bee
buzzing around with
gilded grace and warmth
and an infectious smile and laughter,

we boomers zoomed
into the faraway lands of
Twain, Hemingway, and Poe
Whitman, Emerson, and Thoreau
in a magic velvet carpet
before the advent of
mobiles, google and AI,

when reading was a delight,
and writing without respite,

when photocopying was a luxury,
when internet was still a mystery,

we inhaled the world
of the unknown
in those neatly bound
crisp and clean
voluminous books

and exhaled the joy
of learning beyond boundaries.

Playful and carefree
we would then
skip and hop to the tree-laden
drive-in for a hot *masala dosai*
and a steaming cup of filter coffee
where we met the veteran singer
with a multihued turban
and coaxed him to sing

his classic film song
"Kaalangalil Aval Vasantham
She is spring among the seasons

Kalaigalile Aval Oviyam
She is painting among the art forms

Maadangalil Aval Marghazhi
She is *Marghazhi* among the months

Malargalile Aval Mallikai
She is Jasmine among the flowers"

Written as a prelude to my inaugural talk of 'To America and Back Again' Series on March 21st 2023 at the American Center, Chennai.

The lines from the famous Tamil film song with translation is included to celebrate the legendary singer P B Srinivas.

9. In a World Fraught with Pain

In a world fraught with pain
may the newborn bring healing

Welcome Him. Celebrate Him. Thank Him

In a world caught in vain
may the newborn bring meaning

Welcome Him. Celebrate Him. Thank Him

A meek child born in a manger
in the cold, calm, candid winter.
He carried humility in his heart and
washed his disciples' feet as art.

A gentle friend of sheep and cattle
who surrounded him with warmth
He rose to be the Good Shepherd
to rear the human race with all his heart.

A loving son of simple, kind parents
chose to be the divine messenger.
He turned water into wine at Cana
at the behest of his caring mother.

A born leader who received gifts
from three wise men of the east.
He multiplied fish and bread in plenty
to people who gathered on the mount.

A homeless child got a humble home
because of generous humans
He carried the cross with unconditional love
to show his compassion to millions.

In a world fraught with pain
may the newborn bring healing.

Welcome Him. Celebrate Him. Thank Him

In a world caught in vain
may the newborn bring meaning.

Welcome Him. Celebrate Him. Thank Him

A poem set to tune by my cousin Joe as a tribute to the suffering and the needy on
Christmas 2022

10. She Ached in Happiness

She ached in happiness
at those moments of eternity
how time, seasons and space froze
beyond mere mortal definitions,

where she could see his stinted soul
like the calm flame in a tinted Diya
unruffled by the surrounding storm
yonder human descriptions,

when she felt strangely surreal
at the sound of her heart beat
muttering a soft rhythm in harmony
with the tempo of the universe,

and how she wished to disappear
into thin air like a fairy godmother
carrying those momentary jiffies
in her golden casket towards infinity.

In Love with the Divine Soul Series - Song 1

II Timbre in Brown Bark

11. Birthday at Madison

On a misty morning,
amidst crimson-yellow fall hues,
a day spent far from home,
yet a cherished, chirpy one,
like icing on a piece of carrot cake,
I bought for myself to relish,
with a dash of mother's guilt,

yet feeling on top of the world,
amidst minds from far and wide,
lost in niche thoughts and memories,
of their South Asian tapestries,
drowning themselves in ideas,
dipped in cocoa and coffee,

followed by a stealthy visit to
a random bookstore, named
A Room of One's Own,
to buy Virginia Woolf's classic,
with the same hard-hitting name,

and later to fulfil a childish wish,
to step into the world of
the humble Henry Vilas Zoo,

and return all teary-eyed,
to find little boys hopping around,

who reminded me of my own,
thousands of miles across the pond,
wishing me good on a video call,
with their wide eager smiling eyes,
and a lovely little birthday song.

I wrote these lines after attending the South Asia
Conference at Madison-Wisconsin in Fall 2019

12. Kurinci

Honeybees party
after twelve years hiatus of
Kurinci flowers

red-black soil blend
in passion where water
cascades with free will

women drive parrots
in millet fields singing songs
celebrating pure love.

Tinaiku - Haiku poems on *Kurinci Tinai*

Published in Muse India – the literary E-Journal May-June 2023

13. Mullai

When white *Mullai* buds
glazed in rain reminded him,
she swooned in agony

deer couples on river
banks feel sorry for her when
his journey begins

on late summer noon
clouds gather around to sing
her lover's arrival.

Tinaiku - Haiku poems on *Mullai Tinai*

Published in Muse India – the literary E-Journal
May-June 2023

14. Marutam

Women sing songs to
cast away their burden while
planting paddy stalks.

Standing near a mud wall
she waits for him, feeling pity
for the "other" woman,

as children jump into
muddy ponds to catch tiny
fishes for the day's game.

Tinaiku - Haiku poems on *Marutam Tinai*

Published in Muse India – the literary E-Journal May-June 2023

15. Neytal

Saltiness in warm air
moisture could not compete with
her painful tears,

waves signal courage,
and hope when, even lighthouse forgets
to radiate white beams,

but blue-white lily on
green stalks faithfully celebrate
their love in separation.

Tinaiku - Haiku poems on *Neytal Tinai*

Published in Muse India – the literary E-Journal
May-June 2023

16. Palai

Souls that long to unite,
race on muddy road with sunburnt
soles in deep distress.

Palai flowers in
thorny bushes lend a helping
hand to small reptiles.

Tears of her friend
and mother shields her from
hot air in dry-dreary land.

Tinaiku - Haiku poems on *Palai Tinai*

Published in Muse India – the literary E-Journal May-June 2023

17. Bus Journey to Vettavalam

Nothing has changed much
in twenty to thirty years.

As the rusty barred bus
with half faded *Kural* board
amidst jade-yellow neon lights,
zooms past the windy road
towards Tiruvannamalai,
as the noisy rustic crowd
cheer one another
with guiltless, carefree,
day-to-day stories,
stories, and stories.

A man in madras checks lungi
listens to daily news on his mobile.

A woman in bright red saree
pairing it with *kanagambaram* flowers
has just dialled her mobile
and screen flashes
…calling *Amma*.

The conductor innocently teases
a woman with parrot-green glass bangles
"I will not stop
near the crossroads for you.

What will you do!"

And the woman immediately
responds with a bold gusto
"But don't you remember
you must travel in
this bus route every day!"

Peals of laughter.

A curious woman
with crimson and yellow
plastic wire basket
and brimming smile beside me
eagerly strikes a conversation
"my daughter is studying
in a college".
She smiles like a child.

I ask her what does she study
and in her innocent, rustic tone,
she mutters
"BCom FA"
"What is FA?" I ask her curiously
and the girl beside her
utters confidently "Financial Accounting."

as the bus shriek-stops,
a young mother
with a newborn on her shoulder,

calls out to her neighbor,
with bold-fondness,
"*Anna*, can you get me that bag!"

An unknown stranger
with boundless fraternal feelings
for a newfound sister
fetches her heavy bag
and helps her get off,
to be faithfully acknowledged
by her doting husband
waiting in the bus stop
in cheery-admiration,
"Thanks, *Machaan*!"

and the teeming bus
zooms past the windy road,
amidst jade-yellow neon lights
the noisy rustic crowd
cheer one another
with guiltless, carefree,
day-to-day stories,
stories, and stories.

The poem was written after a faculty-exchange program visit to Loyola College, Vettavalam in Thiruvannamalai District

18. Mother Earth T-r-e-m-o-r-s

Does She

tre-mb-
-le with fear
sh-iv-
-er in cold
f-u-m-
-ble in fury
sh-ud-
-der in pain
qu-i-
-ver in anxiety
st-ut-
-ter in despair

quake in anger?

The ever silent
Earth Mother mur-murs
for a few minutes…

to the minuscule
human race, teaching

Giant lessons of mortality.

Written after being jolted by the news of Turkey Earthquake 2023

19. Child Earth – An Alphabet Poem

All along "Mama Earth"
with respect, we called her
But under our feet and sole
with contempt, we trampled her.
Causing misery and havoc
to her delicate body and soul,
Damaging her calmness,
celestial composure and cool.

Ever unmindful of
her benevolent dealings,
Forging our happiness
on materialistic misgivings,
Gullible to the hubris
of control and conceit,
Humans had developed
as their prime undertaking.

It is high time
we take a gigantic U-turn,
Journeying towards
the untarnished Nature with capital N,
Knowing her goodness and
undaunted fervor with a soul filled-
Love as the only
Guiding and organizing principle,

Mindful of our thoughts,
words, and performances,
Nurturing benevolence
and goodwill to all neglected seeds,
Offering our obeisance
to the newborn divine babe,
Preparing our hearts
and hearths for Child Earth,

Quietly allowing her to rest
comfortably in our hands,
Rocking and singing
a little lullaby to her,
She would wake up
relaxed after the siesta,
To lead us with her elegance
and unconditional love,

Ubiquitous in each
and every life touched by her,
Viewing the future
with refreshing eyes and smile,
Welcoming the guardians
who nourish her with grace,
Xpecting from her green guardians,
protection and untainted care

Yearning for her friends
goodwill and fearless favor,
Z-gen vanguards,
Child Earth is now in your hands.

Written on Earth Day 2023 and read out in the
British Council Poetry Reading Circle

20. Mary Knew Him

He was a fine storyteller
and she was a silent listener.
He...a servant leader
She... a faithful follower.

Sharing his mother's name and grace
she knew their camaraderie
was one of its kind...

She knew he could
calm the raging storm
as a tall magician,

feed the hungry crowd
as a caring mother,

and reprimand
the mighty and proud
with his sensitive deeds
as a learned teacher.

She knew he obeyed
his mother's words with care
and turned water into wine,

treated the Samaritan woman fair
and turned her a better human.

Her heart was in untold joy
when she listened to him
amidst the multitude on the mount,

admired his penance
amidst the burning sands
in the wilderness,

adored his unconditional love
for the lost sheep in distress,

and felt awestruck by
the fisher of men's
face turning red in anger
in the crowded temple.

When the time came
her heart was in untold pain
but for his conscientious words
"Mary...time and space are for mortals."

And she patiently waited…
for his resurrection.

because she knew…

He only did what he said
He only said what he did

And He did what He said.

Mary Magdalene awaiting the resurrection of her Great Friend written on Easter Day 2023.

In Love with the Divine Soul Series - Song 2

III Texture of Blue Skies

21. Haiku in Love

that fine moment when
razor sharp glance tears her heart
into confetti

Haiku a Japanese poetic form with 5-7-5 syllable
pattern in English

22. Breathlessness

breathlessness became
breathtaking when her eyes saw
sunshine-smile at dawn

23. Melted Like Ice

when she searched for him
in the crowd and found, like ice
she melted at once.

24. High Walls

tears welled up her eyes
when he built walls high and high
to hide his feelings.

25. So Many Tears

she had so many
tears to wash her Lord's feet in
complete surrender

26. Love in a Shell

in her heart she loved
him more, when he disciplined
her like oyster pearl.

27. Graceful Glances

busy as gazelle
they skipped and hopped along paths
with graceful gazes.

28. Rock Bottom

like a tight roped rock
in deep well, those memories
bind her soul within.

29. Metamorphosis

seconds twitter, as
caterpillars munch crunchy
leaves before takeoff.

30. She Had Seen His Regal Soul

She had seen His regal soul

smiling like a shimmering star

on a dark, silent, wonder night

even before He firmly knew

He was the chosen King of Kings.

In Love with the Divine Soul Series - Song 3

IV   Dynamics of Gold Sun

31. Time Fools

date, time, month, within year
mismatch sweet melancholic
moments in parting

32. Equalizer

ladder meets balcony
dissolve class disparity in
Romeo Juliet

33. A Mother's Prayer

Understanding things as they are, with noble truths four,
may we root out spring source and end suffering to the core.

With wisdom, choose love, nonviolence, and detachment,
to prune away wild branches of desire and attachment.

Wash away lies, hatred, malice and let noble silence reign,
with pleasant, meaningful words like the benevolent rain.

May peace and respect guide your every little feat my child,
and lead you in honor like the magnificent sun undefiled.

With the least little trouble we could avoid giving others,
by our thoughts, words, deeds like empathetic mothers.

Let us prevent injury through wholesome determination,
may you emerge like moon with goodness and perfection.

Become aware of our body, mind, soul and gently inhale,

may unpleasant wither away like leaves, when trees exhale.

May passion and unrest die, tranquil and serene we gain,

and we surmount sadness and joy and equanimity remain.

Poem written in Couplets based on Buddha's Eight-Fold Path on Buddha Purnima 2023

34. Life Leaves, Death Leaves

I have lived say the leaves,
I have died say the leaves.

I have lived
like tiny-tender
brown-green leaves singing-swinging
on mango trees in summer
when we met.

I have died
like tired-slender
brown-yellow leaves falling-failing
down one by one in autumn
when we part.

I have lived say the leaves,
I have died say the leaves.

35. Tree *Anni*

The tall upright
Almond tree
by the window
reminded of him…

his tree sister
her amicable *Anni*

when in joy
she hugged her,

when in pain
she provided refuge,

when in doubt
she taught her,

when she missed him
she comforted her.

In moments of agony
over separation
his tree sibling
told her,

"My dear
beyond space-time
his soul is within your soul

beyond spirit-matter
he is yours my girl"

She gave a warm hug
to her Sil tree
and felt at peace.

Anni – A term of endearment in Tamil used to call husband's sister.

Inspired by the Tamil *Cankam* poetry motif of love in separation.

36. Blending and Parting

Words betray when
Time dances and sways
to mellifluous tunes of
Love in blending and parting,

beating to rhythms,
ticking to tempos,
patterning pulses,

of arcs beyond the endless.

Silence comforts when
Time dances and sways
to mellifluous tunes of
Love in blending and parting,

sweeping across space,
spanning unseen terrains,
scaling endless vistas,

of bows beyond the boundless.

Inspired by the Tamil *Cankam* poetry motif of love in union and separation.

37. Unpredictable Divine

real like a raving rainfall
bearing seasonal surprises
and showers of sunshine,
Gaia who loves and cares,

is un-
-predict-
-able yet benign
in
compre-
-hensi-
-ble yet Divine.

real like a raging river
not being reduced to matter
like rocks and sand that stay put,
Gaia who loves and cares,

is un-
-predict-
-able yet benign
in
compre-
-hensi-
-ble yet Divine.

real like a razing rainbow

malice beyond her ken
pristine and pure,
Gaia who loves and cares,

is un-
-predict-
-able yet benign
in
compre-
-hensi-
-ble yet Divine.

38. Ma Buddha

~ A Sonnet

She raptures in unconditional love
yet she dons a hero of detachment
By nurturing little ones with a vow
she weans them with discernment

Truth is but an inadequate wording
to define her care for her children
Hate is never easy to find meaning
in her heart nothing short of heaven

She waters timid ones with true courage
when they are really tiny and tender
yet teaches them to let go with age
bent wisdom to put things asunder

A mother is a Buddha who is so dear
a lit-soul makes eight-fold path clear

39. Within Four Walls

A generation glued
to taut tempers,
tense moments,
flitting memories,
dashing flashes,

had to rest for a while,
when the world came
to strange standstill,

when masks managed
to unmask human fragility,

during crumbling times,
coiling around necks
like coir ropes,
in unwilling suspension
of dismay and dispute,

it was subtle stillness
that suckled solace,

when dollops of silence
were served with warmth,
on a platter to
those huddled together
within four walls

without any choice,

who just survived to live.

Remembering the lockdown effect during the Covid 19 Pandemic

40. Mother Tree

As a little girl playfully, but with love, she planted
a little seed, watered it and devotedly chanted,

days became months, months became years
the foliage grew tall and wide with great cheers,

she married and moved to a faraway place,
in a year she delivered and departed with grace.

The Son grew strong with care of his mother divine,
but something he missed that he couldn't define,

the day came, he went in search of the tree shade,
His mother had planted, nurtured as a young maid.

He soon became a learner under Her giant canopy,
to spread far and wide His noblest philosophy.

as a child-seer She had sowed moments of serenity,
for the foreseer to reap moments of serendipity.

She was a divine yantra between Maya and her son
and gave the golden mantra to be the Enlightened One

In Love with the Divine Soul Series - Song 4

The poem carries an imaginary tale of how Siddartha (Buddha's) mother

Maya Devi planted a sapling which grew up into the Bodhi tree which blessed
Gautama Buddha to become the enlightened one.

V   Tempo in Teal Plumes

41. Curry Leaves in Ziplock Pouch

When you leap
across the pond

with hunger
for better pastures
to read and write

palates long for
Ammachi's fried
mustard-chillis in
pink baby radish sambhar,
and smoked pepper fried potatoes
to match steaming
hot long-grained rice.

On sunny afternoons
I skip and hop
along the pavement
to the nearby Indian stores,

where tiny jewel-like
eager mauve shallots
chained in plastic nets,
and deep-green curry leaves
in zip lock pouches,

rise above and silently scream

to be free at last!
to be free at last!

42. Family Reunion – A Prime Poem

Family
reunion

Hearts
redeem
thoughts

Minds
weave in
weave out

Smiles
give light in
times of darkness

Memories
strengthen journeys as they move
forward with grace and warmth

Life
moves on like clear stream forward
carrying magical memories along the way

Thoughts
move around in circles like giant planets
in orbits with beauty, gratitude, and contentment

Hands
that worked together in unison
in moments of distress

celebrate when sweet success paid
off a surprise visit

Feelings
mature with surge of grey hairs
and wrinkles on their faces
eager to harness the remaining days
in this beautiful wide world

Children
remember moments of mischief on Monday mornings
memories of jubilant joy on Friday evenings
days when they fought for pen, pencil
eraser, sharpener, ruler, labels, and glittering stickers

Grandchildren
ask them to narrate stories of their childhood days
from pre-television pre-technology era of innocence
tell them to sing songs seasoned with rustic wit,
rural humour that surpassed all odds

Photographs
naming of firstborn, day she crawled, day she sat
day she stood, the day she walked and fell
captured in black and white, sepia pictures loaded with
emotions, tears, cries, fears of success, failures, betrayals, defeats

A poem in prime numbers. Each stanza is formed by number of words that range from 3 to 39

43. Water Un-homed

Earth holds her gently
like a new born with care,

humans hug her with poise
in every nerve and hair,

trees embrace her fondly
in their bare roots and leaves,

birds bear her lightly
in their tiny feathers and beaks,

where she feels homed.

Taps and pipes clasp her
within grimy, rusty
bars in suspension,

bottles grip her with coldness
in petty, poisoned
plastic prisons,

machines coerce her
taciturnly in boilers
with brute revenge,

dams confine her
within walls like how
mindless patriarchs avenge,

where she feels un-homed.

44. Blue Ticks

when grey ticks
remain grey

her heart pounds
a million times over
in anxiety and fear
as a daughter, mother,
wife, friend
eagerly waiting

for it to turn blue

the liberating hue
of dark deep ocean
and wide sunny sky.

45. Word Child

wrinkles at the centre
and grey hairs at the corner
of your wide forehead

foretells your wisdom
before you speak.

I am cent percent sure,
living words feel blessed
to be pronounced by you,

treated with utmost care
and consideration,

with extreme tenderness
and determination,

uttered with finesse
and fine perfection,

My dear Lord…

I sincerely wish
in my next birth
I would be born your…

…Word.

46. Mélange

As peacocks proudly boast
mottled tails, wings, and feathers
like the three-eyed Dancer,
the eternal Lover of Shakthi,

as early morning dew
on green grass wakes up
to sun's rays piercing prisms
into sparkling spectrum,

as new born pearl eyes
with wonder at her mother's
shell white new home
splashed with polychrome,

as multihued flower petals
huddle around in effeminate joy
and celebrate fresh dawn
in the giant *pookalam*,

with pride my sisters, brothers
go forth and rejoice life
like the three-eyed Dancer,
eternal Lover of Shakthi.

47. Words Heal

I

within a year
we settled in Chennai
my one-year-old sister
was tested jaundice.

we rushed to nearby
10 Rs doctor…
with a smiling face
he prescribed some medicine
and told my little sister,
"drink boiled water *ma*"

And *Amma* sincerely
boiled litres and litres
of water for the next three decades.

II

when I tested
faintly positive,
friends suggested
a gynaecologist's name.

she was a moon goddess
in Kancheepuram silk saree

who took less than five to six
minutes for a consultation.

every month during check-up
I nervously dreaded
the crowd in the clinic.

but when the door opened
and I made way to her altar
with a gracious smile,
she said "you are fine, girl,
nothing to worry."

Mother and I
returned home with a deep sigh.

III

Overpowered by
poetic indulgence,
momentary madness and
unbearable emotional toil
I gobbled up a handful
of paracetamol tablets
on an unfortunate day.

The next minute I saw
my son walking towards me
smiling and asked
"Ma, are you alright?"

the reality struck me hard
and I immediately
tried all the homemade
remedies to wash out
the medicine and angst.

hours later I rushed
to our family physician
and told him the entire story
and blatantly asked
"Am I going to die?"

Never had I seen
an angelic expression
on the old man's face before.

Like the wizard of Oz
he gave me some antidotes
and gently uttered,
"Nothing to worry ma
you are perfectly alright."

I thanked all divine forces in the universe
to bless the gentleman…

and wished "May his tribe increase."

A poem on care-giving, inspired by research in medical humanities.

48. To the Best of the Best

having spent twelve
glorious target years,
honing skills to precision
and chiselling your mind
to fine retention,

with passion as armour,
and persistence as shield,

you were the best of the best,

but when you left us…
without bidding adieu,

mother who housed you
never overcame good grief,

father who guarded you
under his unruffled feathers,
never forgot the fledgling moment
you tripped and fell off the nest,

siblings who saw you
as their first heroes,
still remember glorious days
when you rode high.

come what may
earth goes around

sun rises
seasons change
river flows
rain falls
memories fade
time flies

Oh, the beautiful fire armed soul…

who lived for your aspiration
and died for your honour

martyr of examinations
victim of our society
scion of fate

may you find fullness
of life in spirit
and gently resurrect…
as guardian angel
to guide innocent tiny tots
the best of the best

who are still running
the rat race
in the mad, mad world
of competitions.

An Elegy written in fond memory of an Exam Martyr.

49. Why Read Moby-Dick?

As Ishmael wows us
with a self-introduction,
Ahab vows on his
final whaling malediction,

in the giant canvas
etched by Melville
I vainly search for women.

I find the ocean
a vessel of greedy girth,

of revenge and ruin,
to ill-fated,
one-legged captain,
bidding final adieu
to his wife before
gravely launching
into forbidden seas,

of resource and returns,
to Pequod's first mate,
Starbuck with quiet ambition
but no return,

of refuge and revival,
to the tattooed Queequeg
whose cool coffin saved a frantic life,

I anxiously search
for silences and absences
in the giant volume,
for feminine fervour,
maternal care,
female strength,
and woman power…

After petulantly reading
eighty-plus chapters,
serendipitously
I end up in a colony

of nursing mothers
tending little ones who are
"spiritually feasting upon
some unearthly reminiscence,"
baby whales with delicate fins
safe within the heart of
"the oceanic mother",

unmindful of the mindless humans
with harpoons, spears, and guns,
viciously conspiring to reduce them
into oil, fat, meat, and skin.

I re-read Moby-Dick with

a watchful eye for absences

and an intense ear for silences

to oar against the tide
to seek the lesser-known yet
promising "stranger world" below

"this wondrous world upon the surface."

Wrote this poem after I delivered a talk on Melville's magnum opus 'Moby-Dick' from an eco-critical perspective. I have quoted some phrases from the novel to celebrate the great classic.

50. Fasting is Feasting

Dear Lord,

Fasting is feasting

Have you ever thought

Love as fasting!

But when your loved one

teaches you to fast

Fasting is feasting

Love is fasting

Dear Lord,

Fasting is feasting

In Love with the Divine Soul Series - Song 5

VI   Rhythm of Red Roses

51. Inland Letters

Ammachi's handwritten letter
in a ruled notebook paper
with yellowed edges
carrying magic words of love,

De Mello's letter to *Appa*
congratulating him on the
birth of his first baby girl
sending hugs and kisses
to the little one
still carries the warmth within me

Appa's post cards during
summer vacation in Kodaikanal

Amma's inland letters
with rounded Tamil letters
to her sisters
perfectly reciprocated
by *Chithi*'s beautiful
handwritten ones
discussing mundane matters
about dried *vadagam* on the terrace
and her irregular periods.

Periamma's affectionate
baggage on paper
describing yellow and black
flowered Poonam silk sarees

Athai's crisp and clear
sentences reflecting
the professor's poetic candour
in *Centamil* syntax

are emissaries of love beyond compare.

Remembering the habit and culture of writing letters in the 1980s.

52. Mad Musings

One stormy day
Muse and Madness
came together
to meet me on the way.

Caught unaware
by mysterious monsoon spell
I got drenched in nectar,
swooned in love
like a cocooned caterpillar
squirming in sugary pain.

My soul leapt up
like a gazelle
hit by piercing arrow gaze,
with words beyond measure
to sing heart's content

of infinite journeys
voyaged in a millisecond,
catapulting across
passionate trajectories
from one planet to another
across galaxies galore,

swirling around in a frenzy
like drunken bees

in a honeycomb,
words at times failing
memorable musings,
at other times
madness outweighing
poetic moorings.

In a forlorn boat caught in
stormy seas with yearning eyes
I faithfully
looked up to my Muse
and there

you stood tall and upright
with a beacon of light
guiding me safe and sound
across sun kissed horizons.

After the storm came calm

Madness left with grace
and Muse chose to stay.

53. Eyes Never Lie

Her eyes never lied
His eyes never denied.

But

words wore clinical masks
to prevent infectious fervour,
robed in armour and shields
to protect heart's candour…

words played hide and seek
to discourage and dissuade,
love wrought by the weak
to disallow and persuade…

words failed to carry through
the emotions unpredictable
and swayed like a silly shrew
with feelings uncountable…

But

Her eyes never lied
His eyes never denied.

54. Figures of Silence

Learning hard to become
fluent in language of silence

that carry a multi-million
unspoken honest words,

with similes like diamond
studded within coals,

metaphors of gold laden rose whorls,

hyperbole of silver arc that leaps up
to touch the glimmering moon,

oxymoron of bitter sweet memories untold,

that gently rhyme with the rhythm

of the unfathomed universe,
that fathoms my love for you

carefully wrapped up
in arms of graceful calm.

A poem on silence using figures of speech

55. Tea for the Soul

when we are weary, worn, and weak

Tea embraces our tired, torn soul
with warmth of a loving mother,

dipped in farm, fresh fragrance
of minty-cardamom, leafy flavour
effervescent with cinnamon love,

binding little broken heart pieces
of China, gently gold-glued together,

mending great wall of faith forever.

56. Winter Solstice

the shortest day
of Sun meeting the Earth

yet a strongest one,

as his tender radiance
touch green-red leaves
at cherubic dawn,

with a graceful visage,
the determined daisy

looks up to him in all wonder
and greets him in all splendour,

in soulful silence…

which words cannot measure
within a jewelled jiffy moment.

57. Plant Love

Once upon a time the red hibiscus twig
I planted with love and hope, grew taller than me,
bearing hundred and one flowers…

the guava tree, that my little brother watered every
day, at early morn, grew tall, to give enough shade,
when we were out to play at sunny noon…

the henna plant stood canopied, dense, and
unrestrained, carrying a festive aroma all day long…

the curry leaves branched out with heady, herby
fragrance and spread its fervour around…

all in the sparrow nesting backyard of my countryside
type house, in the middle of the city, which planted
love and hope in me to care for plants.

An experimental prose poem based on childhood
memories.

58. May the Day

> May the day abundantly bring,
> to human hands that deftly sing,
>
> hope to those who sincerely toil,
> joy to those born in this noble soil,
>
> beyond caste, creed, and gender,
> class, community, race asunder,
>
> whose tidy sweat of tired brow,
> waters roots of our society to grow,
>
> stemming out stalks of refuge,
> branching out leaves of courage,
>
> flowering forth without any reserve,
> yielding fruits, they duly deserve,
>
> May the day abundantly bring,
> to human hands that deftly sing.

Acknowledging the laborers who build the world on May Day

59. Flowers are Silent Prayers

Flowers are silent prayers

with cool, calm composure,
tethering earth with sun,

ferrying tenderness and warmth,
lilting hopes and cheers,
amidst struggles and pain,

painting her world rich and bright,
with multitudinous hues,

of magic and miracles

with a simple smile
of peace.

60. Gifts

She connects and reconnects
God the Father and Mother
with the mighty God the Son
weaving threads of wisdom
knowledge and understanding
intertwined with fragrant
flowers of fortitude
interspersed with
cool colours of counsel
and pretty pearls of piety
with fear of the Lord

In Love with the Divine Soul Series - Song 6

VII   Harmony in Black Woods

61. sTree

she remains grounded
connecting earth with sky…

with her soul full of grace,
magnifying Her good Lord,
and exalting Him with praise.

day in and day out…

wishing every ant and dragonfly
amidst mist and rain…

blessing every bee and butterfly
during bright sunshine…

connecting soil with clouds…

with her soul full of grace,
magnifying Her good Lord,
and exalting Him with praise.

Stree refers to a woman. The word also has tree embedded in it. The poem acknowledges the woman-tree proximity in cultures close to nature. It takes a cue from Mary's Magnificat that begins with the line "My soul magnifies the Lord".

62. When I Die Don't Bury Me

when I die don't bury me
as it is customary,
because my soul is a burning bush
all day turning me into ashes
consuming every second…

pain is a pleasant-penalty,
suffering is sour-sweet,
so, cremate me and
let the fire quench fire…

from the ashes may rise a phoenix
only to burn me alive again and again,
with perennial passion
my soul eternally waiting for you…

place a bouquet of red roses
on my tomb that would remind me
of your blushing face
and smiling eyes
that nobody else in this
whole wide world has ever seen

and my soul would rest in peace.

Wrote this poem for a poetry workshop on the theme of "Love and Pain".

63. Saint of the Slums

To those who are in abysmal need,
He aids them find the dear lost one;
their every single word he does heed
when folks feel they are nearly done;

Carrying new born babe in his gentle arm,
in slums and ghettos across the moor;
with Mother's rosary grace and charm,
He finds a petite home amidst the poor;

Crowns and sceptres are never his lot,
but he holds an army with fine brigade;
A rescuer of torn-to-atone and their sort,
liberating them from every barricade;

He is the humble Don of the downtrodden.
An unassuming, meek saint of the subaltern.

A sonnet written for St Antony, patron saint of the subaltern people living in slums and ghettos.

64. Life Sentence

Life is a sentence

every tiny
word
follows
another
in
a
row
a single step forward.

meet with a comma,
and with gusto we proceed,

meet with a full stop
and be dead and buried.

Commas are natural bridges
above a silent sublime stream.

Full stops are tall dams of fear
that damn mighty rivers
into extinction and tears.

Commas are gentler creatures
with a heart so warm.

Full stops are cruel monsters

that shock us with false alarm.

Commas are peacemakers,
Full stops are piece makers.

May a full stop tear out
into a comma, for us to pause a second,

and may the sentence continue forever,

A poem built on punctuation marks, comma and full stop and experimental syntax.

65. Bitter Sweet

Oxymoron made Verse

Life is
bitter sweet,

setting us
alone together,

in a journey of
static flow,

where
cruel kindness,

incensed with
deafening silence,

blurs
bright smoke

from
cold fire,

solemnly exchanging
sad smiles,

to survive
as living dead,

loaded with
memories catapulting,

across
borderless boundaries,

as dandelions
heavy light,

nods a
noiseless sound

as notes of
wordless psalms.

A poem on the use of Oxymoron, the figure of speech with irony, humour, and satire.

66. She Began Fasting

She began fasting
with thoughts of pure melted gold.

She began fasting
with words of wisdom truly untold.

She began fasting
to do great deeds of graceful might.

with Saint Joseph
her mindful muse, chivalrous knight.

67. Lingua Myopia

Don't dare to decode *Anbu*
with your myopic lenses…
you will only see a partial eclipse,
that fits your limited eyes.

Don't dare to decode *Aram*
with your technical toolkit…
you will only fail to derive,
the theory of gravity in depth.

Don't dare to decode *Akam*
with scary, strategic whims…
that can never ever measure,
the density of heart and earth.

Don't dare to decode *Arul*
the eternal grace that resides…
in all loving souls, big-small, their,
relativity unmeasured in any labs.

The Tamil words *Anbu* (meaning love, affection, friendship, care etc) *Aram* (justice, charity, benevolence, magnanimity etc), *Akam* (meaning heart, home, world, face etc) and *Arul* (grace, elegance, beauty, blessing etc) are consciously used to drive home the difference between languages and emotions.

68. Love Gift-Wrapped in Memory

A tall tree born of this red soil
carries with her a warm memory
of a benevolent, nurturing seed,
a solid rock in her tender heart
on which…

her evergreen home is built upon.

A tiny bird born of the crimson skies
carries with her a warm memory
of a wholesome, feathery nest,
a solid rock in her tender heart
on which…

her boundless home is built upon.

A dusky child born of a doting mother
carries with her a warm memory
of a selfless, unconditional womb,
a solid rock in her tender heart
on which…

her ever-loving home is built upon.

A loving woman born of this sunny Earth
carries with her a warm memory
of a sober, sublime, supreme soul,

a solid rock in her tender heart
on which…

her everlasting home is built upon.

69. Breaking the Walls

God with a Holy Name
saw from above,
some sad and troubled,
some haughty and proud,

sitting on either side of a vanity wall
muttering ineffective prayers
in an ascending acrid tone
on stairways to heavens…

on one side the guileless,
were groaning and moaning
in pain, over their thin gruel
that didn't fill,

even half their children's gut
the whole tiresome day.

on the other, the guiltless
were boasting and drowning,
in vain-pride pleasures
that didn't still,

teach them satisfaction
in every word they say.

amidst the meaningless babble

they incessantly uttered
God felt something wasn't right.
He decided to forgive
the sins of the rich,
and save the poor
from their testing ditch.

He sent some angels down
to hammer the hubris wall into pieces,
and break the thousand years old
caste-castle-curse to create
His Kingdom on Earth.

to fulfil the soulful Wish and Prayer
of His only dear Son and Saviour

Inspired by Lord's Prayer 'Our Father' and remarkable episodes of Jesuit history when they broke down the walls that separated the high caste and low caste in churches in the 19th century,

70. Tiny Little Particles of You

Dear Lord,

on a wild windy day...

tiny little particles of you
fell into my tired eyes
and dammed it with tears...

then slowly descended
into my parched throat with
insinuating wry coughs
dancing in distress for a while...

and like a king entering
the royal chambers, you ascended
the majestic throne of my heart...

and in an unexpected moment
captivated me deep into
your chains of cruel charm
as an eternal prisoner
to the end of doomed days.

I choose to be your slave forever my Lord!

In Love with the Divine Soul Series - Song 7

VIII   Melody of Purple Petals

71. Thorn Crowns

Thorn crowns and whip cracks
are nothing new
in the painful way of the cross.

Lord you are there
to guide me along the rocky path!

Lord you are there
to lift me when I stumble and fall!

Lord you are there
to lead me through the pitch dark!

Lord you are there
to protect me when I feel badly lost!

Thorn crowns and whip cracks
are nothing new
in the painful way of the cross.

72. Oh…!

someone becomes our hero,
when we find ourselves a zero!

there is cent percent no ego,
when our self we truly forego!

simple and sweet we gently let go,
of things fondly we cannot out do!

which lends a star-studded glow!
in our hearts to make love grow!

Celebration of Zero with the sound of O

73. Distant Cousins

Mosquitoes
are Hummingbirds and Bees,

tiny distant, dicey cousins,
with ready reckoner ringtones,

busy like brother bees,
in black-gold party tees,

chirpy like brisk birdies,
in blue-green lacy sleeves,

singing a million songs,
of earth's rich histories,

reverberating tiny tunes,
of universal mysteries,

aligning with silvery stars,
and mellow moon miracles,

celebrating their bestie goals,
and love for their Gaia-given roles.

74. Tears are Uncountable Words

Tears are uncountable words
that hold letters of untold pain,

with every sanguine drop deftly
turned into pure distilled water,

in dammed, flood gated eyes
outpouring into clear cascades,

seasoned with the salt of earth
to form a sweet-sad, sacred ode,

which is neither ever maimed nor
mildly misunderstood, yet silently,

proclaim a tiny, tender love-lore,
that is mightier than the universe.

Inspired by the *Kural* "*Anbirkum undo adaikunthaal*" meaning there are no gate locks that can stop the tears of the heart that is in love and the love motifs from *Akam* poetry.

75. Where There is Divine Light

Dear Shepherd,

where your love
is like bamboo flute
carrying million tunes!

where your warmth
is like green grass
as silky velvet carpets!

where your knowledge
is like sturdy staff
that guides and prunes!

where your honesty
is like golden garb
which joyfully protects!

where your prudence
is like silver turban
springing with goodwill!

where your courage
is like shimmering sword
guarding me from danger!

where your faith
is like glistening armour

keeping me away from every ill!

where your Soul shines
like the Divine Light
and leads me forever…

there is nothing I shall want!

with love,

A little lamb

A pastoral letter written by a lamb to a shepherd inspired by the shepherd boy Krishna and shepherd boy David and his Psalm 23 'The Lord is my Shepherd'.

76. Window in the Attic

Holding his hands
I would cheerily climb up
the wooden stairs
with a thumping sound…
and find neatly primed attic
well-kempt by my *Ammachi*
for her dear son-in-law…

He would sit there
for hours peering through
the small iron-barred window
that providentially had
an extended whitewashed sill,
his standby study table
to read and write
throughout the day
during the summer vacation.

Standing on my toes
I would eagerly look at
the misty world outside the window
and there was "Alas!
a pricey piece of heaven on earth!"

Tree-laden dense green
mountains stretching
beyond the sun-lit horizon,

deep blue sky dotted
with sparkling white clouds
moving like an enlightened ascetic
uninterrupted by the
chirping home sparrows,
black and gold painted mynahs,
and the munchkin screams
of my cousins asking me
to get down and play with them,

name, place, animal, thing!

"Name, place, animal, thing" is a popular indoor game played by the children during summer vacation in the 1990s.

77. Nature's Fury

Trees are disappearing into thin, grey, sad-smoke!
Raging seas and oceans are rising tall and high!
Land is trembling amidst their crazy, mindless havoc!
Glaciers are tearfully melting into brittle sheets of ice!

Plastic beads mercilessly choke-rip fishes deeply-dire!
Birds miss out on humble daily dose of petite-prey!
Animals fatigue into fits, fumble down in forest fire!
Bees in search of flowers turn mad on scorching day!

But here is man fighting for his own lot and money!
Losing his useless senses on the dark, endless futile!
With a list of lust, greed, selfishness, ego, and vanity!
Knowing too well but forgetting he is bit too fragile!

With patience, She gives a chance to mend his path!
Sooner or later, she will incarnate into being of wrath!
Nature will reprimand and hit him hard and aloud!
For all his faulty-fickled words of being rude-proud!

78. Mettā Tunes of Gaia

Rivulets softly reverberate
along tiny pebbles and stoic rocks

playing to Mettā tunes of Gaia

Carnations gently celebrate
camaraderie of caring honey bees

dancing to Mettā tunes of Gaia

Hummingbirds warmly habituate
new feisty fledglings with hope

swinging to Mettā tunes of Gaia

Mother's heart firmly resonates
with her child's heart beats

singing to Mettā tunes of Gaia

Written as a Prayer to Mother Earth. Mettā is a Buddhist term for benevolence, loving-friendship, or kindness to life around.

79. Anam Cara (Soul Friend)

His wisdom stands like a rock,
blazing bright with tenderness,
on a star dust misty miracle.

With clarity like a flowing rivulet,
amidst green plant pals cheering,
Her journey of thousand light years.

With armed guidance like dewy arc,
sprinkling hope on wishful wings,
of swirling busy bees and wasps.

Understanding like cool rain cloud,
drawing breath from ocean depths,
that sing praise of a soul in love.

80. She Chose Silence

having lost faith in man-made words

which she tried to say,
but poorly did betray…

that failed to express, what she purely felt,
as a caring, cordial, sensitive, simple,
harmless, harmonious, gentle, but now,
a tired and worn-out soul…

She chose Silence
as her convoy
once again…

and now the unsaid and the unheard,
are more musical,
to her ears, mind and heart…

carrying the gift of sublime…
through infinite time…

connecting blazing stars of the skies,
with the depths of the darkest seas.

Let music of silence rule forever!
Let the supreme soul live forever!

the unsaid and the unheard,

are more musical,
to his ears, mind and heart…

carrying the gift of sublime…
through infinite time…

connecting blazing stars of the skies,
with the depths of the darkest seas.

Let music of silence rule forever!
Let the supreme soul live forever!

In Love with the Divine Soul Series - Song 8

IX   Beat to Silver Streams

81. Mother Dear

orphaned as a child
homeless as a mother,
She knew
what suffering meant…

which makes Her
and Her Son

living Waters of grace…
to empathise with the distressed,

and care for the oppressed

82. A Beacon of Wisdom

Dear Lord,

In the desert's cold and endless night,
you are the star that leads me through!

a lighthouse shining, strong and bright,
in research's depths, you guide what's true!

your calm reflects the skies afar,
though countless tasks weigh on your mind!

you bear the load without a scar,
and yet, in peace, your heart I find.

In Love with the Divine Soul Series - Song 9

83. Maya and Her Muse

pure, pristine, white light
that drives away darkness
of ignorance and impurities
enlightened her mind womb,

to create word poems of love
and care that was far beyond
material, mundane, ephemeral
but truly ethereal and eternal,

and Maya was born
to her muse son Buddha!

Historically, Maya Devi is the mother of Buddha. In these lines of verse, Gautama Buddha is considered the muse and Maya, the poet is considered his child.

84. The Little Black Bird

the little black bird
sings a lonely song,
on a foggy dark day,
unmindful of the
blessings that are in store,

in the next spring…

living within a miracle
that sparkles like a diamond,
radiating rays of light,
breaking the prism open,
and dispersing into
rainbow colours,

when my heart sings
in ecstasy…

85. I am Home

Dear Lord,
after a hazardous journey…
I am home…
after a disastrous dream…
I am home…
after a risky recovery…
I am home…
after a thunderous blow
I am home…
after a meandering maze
I am home…
after a mad detour
I am home…

In Love with the Divine Soul Series - Song 10

86. Birthing

Woman's writing is from her mind,
may or may not be,
fastened to her womb,
a home for life,

but truly twined to her loving heart,
a hallowed hearth,
that tenderly births and nourishes
other lives with perpetual care,

with a vital sentient caring-cord
of nurture beyond mortal compare…

87. Refuge

even when they whipped me black and blue
and crowned me with cruel thorns,

I was numb to pain!

even when they laid me bare on the cross
in crimson hue and drove me with deceit,

I was dumb to ache!

but now, human hubris hounds me like hell!

when I see baffle-eyed children
running away terrified from bombshells!

when I hear teary-troubled mothers
wailing away for their dear-dead ones!

when I feel nature
mourning away at the loss
of her feathery friends and flocking herds

I feel an excruciating pain
in my chilling back bones,

a sharp piercing hurt
in rivetted scars
of my worn-out palms and legs,

and I regret being born
in that complicated soil...

as a simple, unblemished soul,
in a humble manger,
two thousand years ago.

And now with remorse...

we seek refuge in you, dear Mothers!

Wrote this poem for the British Council Poetry Reading Circle on the theme 'Regret/Refuge'

88. Magni-Psalm

Dear Lord,

My soul magnifies the Lord
who wakes me up
every newborn day dawn!

My soul magnifies the Lord
who jolts me up
with every complacent morn!

My soul magnifies the Lord
who comforts me
with His arms of tender care!

My soul magnifies the Lord
who gently leads me
through valley of dark despair!

My soul magnifies the Lord
who nourishes me
with His fruits of Holy Spirit!

My Soul magnifies the Lord
who enlightens me
true value of love delight!

In Love with the Divine Soul Series - Song 11

Inspired by the Magnificat.

89. Bird Song

Her songs carry dewy-dreams
of twinkling forest-fireflies,
fearing the sunny-dawn
and hiding amidst green-moss,
telling tribal-tales of truth
to the half-buried seeds,
that await the first-rain
to give out their gift in green.

90. Her Lord, Her Boss

amidst busy dog days,
little one gets shooed away,
by her Lord, her Boss,
as she scampers out,
with smiling eyes, pretty paws,
and crystal-clear, kind soul,
like a handful of glossy marbles
silently rolling out into grassy lawn,
without any grumbles,
frowns or fumbles,
because she loved him,
and she knew he loved her too.

In Love with the Divine Soul Series - Song 12

X Meter of White Clouds

91. Martians and Venusians

Martians are not new to emerald Earth,
they pose as tall righteous rulers of race;
many aeons since sapphire dot's birth,
holding reins of horses at faster pace;

Venusians quietly dealt with seed deeds,
nurturing offsprings with tenderest care;
attending to every one's fondness needs,
patiently awaiting their equal share;

Gaia had solemnised their first meeting,
with pure crystal-clear dear spring waters;
and gentle wind drums softly breath beating,
to the soul songs of her foster daughters;

Time wheel has revolved since then far beyond!
Mom still waits for them to resolve peace bond!

A sonnet inspired by the book 'Men are from Mars, Women are from Venus'

92. Muse Soul

My muse doesn't know sadly,
the value of His supreme soul,
that burns like a gentle flame,
on the moonlit mountain top.

His sublime self shines through,
like a tender miracle only to me,
unaffected by worldly designs,
he often desperately tries to fit in.

He dazzles in galaxies across,
Milky Way with infinite goodness,
brimming over his radiant spirit,
alas! as unaware mere mortal man.

With grandeur in epic thoughts,
splendour in taste, His graceful,
sacred self is visible only to me,
he sadly misses in poor company.

Across time and space, a day He,
would discover His incandescent,
Soul that inspired a kindred soul,
to journey through poetic universe.

and write this mellifluous lithe ode,
with fine words dipped in liquid gold.

In Love with the Divine Soul Series - Song 13

93. Sober Silence

A Children's Rhyme

Nature does not have this tilted trait
in leaves, buds, or flowers straight!

amidst busy bees and agile ants
there are no humbug sycophants!

wiling away precious, bare moments
on empty words, hollow comments!

that winged and finned never advise
Time to wither away with tricky lies!

Oh, how well hummingbirds sweetly sing
hailing a promising a regal rainbow ring!

or rooted trees exalt committed clouds
to do duly duties without worthless words!

wish the wordy decay as dead fall leaves
manuring forest floor as truthful weaves!

to wake up the sacred in sleeping-soul sapiens
to spread their blazing aura as earth citizens!

94. Jesus of Nazareth

He saw his mother storing stories,
along with seeds in their barn
which he dispensed in soulful style
when time was really ripe.

He spoke to the trees and lil sheep
waters and fishes, skies, and birds
like His mother and her friends
who knew sister Nature so well.

He healed the sick and injured
fed the hungry and thirsty poor
like the benevolent earth mother
rejuvenating life from living dead.

He loved everyone who loved him
and cared for those who hated him
as he was a gift born of the Word
wrapped in divine love for this world.

The poem is written as an answer to the question, "Is He an Ecofeminist?"

95. King of Kings

When you rode high on the pinnacle
as king of kings with heart so simple!

I stood afar with soulful humble pride
amidst lilies of the valley on riverside!

As green palms curtained you along
cheerful praises drowned birds' song!

I yearned to see your graceful visage
that serenely bore a divine message!

A gentle glance I longed in patience
surrendering with a mindful penance!

Like a miracle little donkey drew near
Finally saw your smiling eyes so dear!

Written on Palm Sunday April 2025

In Love with the Divine Soul Series - Song 14

96. Ellipsis Psalm

I am grateful... ... ... Lord

... ... blessed ... ...

... ... fear ... ... courage

... ... weak ... ... strength

... ... struggle ... ... comfort

... ... doubt ... ... faith ... ...

You ... ... path ... ... hand

... ...heart ... ...

I ... ... music ... ...

... ... peace

Ellipsis is the omission from speech or writing of a word or words that are superfluous.

In Love with the Divine Soul Series - Song 15

97. Chocolate Mothers

Hearts that care for you
like hot melted fresh cocoa
bean dark chocolate.

98. Ration Shop

sad faces, hungry cans,
torn clothes, heat, perspiration,
tired eyes hoping.

99. Town Bus

early morning, cool
breeze, empty seats, lonely streets
stirring in great speed.

100. Feathered Mother

rainbow colours merge
in her soft coat, she feeds young
ones under blue sky.

101. Pollution

fishes, crabs, corals
in Mediterranean
intone plastic blues!

102. A Kind Word

silence carries kind
countless words, twinkling like stars
on cold winter skies!

103. Lucky Dip

Serendipity
a tiny little dip
within Serenity!

104. Delhi Beckons

Aura of tall men and women who led
the nation lingers in fort walls of red,

misty mornings tell taller histories
of faith-hope in human ministries,

diverse crowds from every corner
own the place with unique honour,

as a diamond on crown, She shines
with full bright offers, in gold mines,

yet, Her humble lawns in garden green
homes birds and flowers, truly divine.

Remembering a visit to Delhi for the first time to attend the Fulbright interview in November 2018.

105. Find Her Deep Soul

for a woman has faith in the unseen soul
as a mother, who saw the complete being
in the tiny life, before he started breathing,

find her deep soul and you will feel *Shakthi!*

for a woman has hope in the invisible soul
as a farmer, who saw the wholesome tree
in the minute seed, before green is set free,

find her deep soul and you will feel *Ahimsa!*

for a woman has trust in the unfettered soul
as an architect. who saw a great leader in you
in a word of nobility, that created her anew,

find her deep soul and you will feel *Shanthi*

In Love with the Divine Soul Series - Song 16

www.ingramcontent.com/pod-product-compliance
Lightning Source LLC
LaVergne TN
LVHW091538070526
838199LV00002B/110